CREATIVE LIVES

FRANK LLOYD WRIGHT

HAYDN MIDDLETON

www.heinemann.co.uk/library
Visit our website to find out more information about **Heinemann Library** books.

To order:
 Phone 44 (0) 1865 888066
Send a fax to 44 (0) 1865 314091
Visit the Heinemann Bookshop at www.heinemann.co.uk/library to browse our
catalogue and order online.

First published in Great Britain by Heinemann Library, Halley Court, Jordan Hill, Oxford
OX2 8EJ, a division of Reed Educational and Professional Publishing Ltd. Heinemann is a
registered trademark of Reed Educational & Professional Publishing Ltd.

OXFORD MELBOURNE AUCKLAND JOHANNESBURG BLANTYRE
GABORONE IBADAN PORTSMOUTH NH (USA) CHICAGO

Designed by Tinstar Design (www.tinstar.co.uk)
Originated by Ambassador Litho Ltd.
Printed and bound in Hong Kong/China

ISBN 0 431 13981 4
05 04 03 02 01
10 9 8 7 6 5 4 3 2 1

British Library Cataloguing in Publication Data
Middleton, Haydn
Frank Lloyd Wright. – (Creative Lives)
1.Wright, Frank Lloyd, 1867-1959 – Juvenile literature
2.Architects – United States – Biography – Juvenile literature
I.Title
720.9'2

Acknowledgements
The Publisher would like to thank the following for permission to reproduce photographs:
Arcaid: Richard Bryant p50, Alan Weintraub pp15, 16, 54, John Edward Linden p54, Lewis
Gasson p33, Natalie Tepper pp19, 31; Avery Architectural and Fine Arts Library, Columbia
University: p42; Chicago Historical Society: p51; Frank Lloyd Wright Archives: Associated
Press p37, Gurdjieff Institute p23; Frank Lloyd Wright Preservation Trust: pp4, 10, 13, 14, 21,
27, 38; John Donat Photography: p48; Kobal: p46; Michael Freeman: p43; Nancy
Stone/Chicago Tribune: p9; Paul Rocheleau: pp5, 19, 20, 23, 41, 47; State Historical Society
of Wisconsin: pp6, 8, 24, 26, 28, 34, 44, 52, Art Institute of Chicago p29. Extract on p51:
Copyright © 1969 Paul Simon. Used by permission of the Publisher: Paul Simon Music.Cover
photograph reproduced with permission of Corbis.

Our thanks to Professor Gregory K. Hunt for his comments in the preparation of this book.

Every effort has been made to contact copyright holders of any material reproduced in
this book. Any omissions will be rectified in subsequent printings if notice is given to
the Publisher.

Any words appearing in the text in bold, **like this**, are explained in the Glossary.

CONTENTS

THE GREATEST ARCHITECT WHO EVER LIVED?

Some people are so creative they cannot confine themselves to a single area of activity. Frank Lloyd Wright (1867–1959) was one of those people. He will always be remembered as a fine and revolutionary architect. In a recent national survey, the American Institute of Architects saluted him as 'the greatest American architect of all time'. But he also designed furniture, fabrics, dinnerware and linens, and he was a world-famous author and lecturer, too.

Appearances mattered greatly to Frank Lloyd Wright – not least his own. His highly dramatic outfits helped to emphasize his utter individuality.

A passionate, patriotic, highly industrious man, Wright saw himself as a kind of missionary for his own, often **radical**, ideas and principles. Not everyone approved of him or his work, but few doubted that he made a powerful impact on American life. His constant dream was to create a new architecture; one that did not simply copy old European models, but instead reflected and celebrated the way that **democratic** American people lived. 'Whether people are fully conscious of this or not,' he once said, 'they actually derive **countenance** and sustenance from the "atmosphere" of the things they live in or with. They are rooted in them just as a plant is in the soil in which it is planted.'

'Frank Lloyd Wright was the greatest architect who ever lived. We know this because he told us. He was certainly convinced of it and, although not always appreciated in his lifetime, he probably has as good a claim as anyone to being the most famous architect, at least of modern times. His fame came partly from his ability to **mythologize** himself and his astute self-portrayal as the great defender of what he saw as the American traditions of freedom and **untrammelled** creativity. It also, of course, sprang from his brilliantly original, often inspired buildings.'
Edwin Heathcote, *Financial Times*, July 2000.

Wright was the architect of this house, Fallingwater, in Pennsylvania, built in 1936. It has been called the most famous house ever designed for non-royalty.

A restless genius

Wright lived for almost a hundred years, and he seldom wasted any of his time. He was born just two years after the end of the American Civil War; he died two years after the launching of the first Sputnik satellite into space. In between, he designed no fewer than 1141

Wright was almost worshipped by many of his apprentices and admirers. 'One felt in the presence of a great man,' said Herbert Fritz, a **draftsman**. 'He'd either shock you or amuse you. He was 200 per cent alive.'

Who is the fairest?

Wright was seen by some as a vain, arrogant man. In his later years, he could seem extremely self-absorbed and self-assured. A young relative of his, Jeanne T. Bletzer, said of him: 'Of course he was vain. He'd be talking to me and if there was a mirror in the room he'd be looking into that the whole time and not at me...'

works. These included many houses, hotels, offices, churches, bridges, museums, synagogues and schools. Out of these, 532 resulted in completed works – and 409 of them still stand. One of his lasting achievements was to free Americans from the **Victorian** 'boxes' of 19th century housing, and help to make **open-plan** living possible, with rooms that flowed and opened out into one another. But he was never the kind of man to sit back and simply enjoy his success, in his private life or in his work. 'The important thing to grasp about Wright,' said the British architect Peter Matthews, who once served him as an apprentice, 'is that nothing was ever finished. It was the ideas that interested him; the actual building was secondary.'

One idea that obsessed Wright was that buildings should grow naturally from their surroundings. This arose from his delight in finding patterns and rhythms in the natural world around him. As a boy, he taught himself to see even the branches of trees as natural **cantilevers**. Many years later, he must have had them in mind when he designed the wonderful cascading cantilevers for the Fallingwater house (see picture on page 5).

Throughout his life, he praised the beauty of native materials, and strove to create an '**organic**' kind of architecture, in which the man-made would harmonize happily with the environment. He urged his apprentices to 'study nature, love nature, stay close to nature. It will never fail you.' There was no possibility that anything this idealistic architect designed should be merely 'functional'. 'A building is not just a place to be,' he proclaimed. 'It is a way to be.'

But a man with such strong views was bound to upset some people. He knew how provocative and even aggressive he could be. 'I've always wanted to take the dust off people,' he once laughed. In addition, the way he lived his life – especially his relationships with women – caused a great deal of scandal. Many men have been called larger than life. Frank Lloyd Wright – who stood only 174 centimetres (5'8½") tall – was such a man by any measure you care to take.

A CELTIC CHILDHOOD

Frank Lloyd Wright was a patriotic all-American hero, yet he had a great deal of British blood in him. His mother, Anna Lloyd Jones, was born into a large Welsh family that emigrated to the USA. They settled in the valley near Spring Green, Wisconsin. Anna's own mother – a deeply religious woman like all the Lloyd Joneses – spoke only Welsh until she died.

Wright's father, William Cary Wright, was an American, but also had a British background. Members of his family believed that they could trace their ancestry back to Saxon times in the 6th century AD. William was fourteen years older than Anna, and when they met he was a musician studying to become a church preacher. He was also a widower with three children.

New to the USA, members of the Lloyd Jones clan lived in Wisconsin farmhouses, like this one. Their family motto was 'Truth Against the World'.

Wright's exact birthplace is a mystery. The house was certainly in or around Richland Center, Wisconsin, and some experts believe it was this one. Although lacking many modern comforts, the Wright home was neat and tastefully decorated.

Anna and William married in 1866, but there is some confusion about the year their first child was born. Although he later gave his birthdate as 8 June 1869, Frank Lloyd Wright was actually born two years earlier.

The Lloyd Jones family had moved across the Atlantic in 1844, when Wright's mother was a young girl. She made sure her own children knew all the myths and legends from her old country. Wright took his **Celtic** Welsh ancestry very seriously: he later changed his second name, Lincoln, to Lloyd, and his own famous home was named Taliesin after a character from a medieval Welsh story. But he visited Wales just once.

A nomadic early life

Wright's parents had two more children: Jane in 1869 and Maginel in 1877. Their father moved the family around a lot in his search for work as a musician and preacher. The young Wright spent parts of his boyhood in Rhode Island, Iowa and Massachusetts. This did not help his schooling, and there is no proof that he ever graduated from high school. But wherever the family went, they were usually short of money, and this put a great strain on the relationship between Wright's parents.

When Wright was eleven, the family moved to Madison, Wisconsin. Here they were close to the Lloyd Joneses. Wright would spend each summer on the farm of his uncle, James Lloyd Jones. 'As a boy,' he later wrote, 'I learned to know the ground plan of the region in every line and feature... I still feel myself as much a part of it as the trees and birds and bees are, and the red barns.'

He would never lose his love for this part of the world. But his stern relatives made him work on the farm until he dropped and when Wright protested, they simply told him to 'add tired to tired'. This was a **maxim** that Wright never forgot.

Wright at the age of ten, shortly before his father moved the family to Madison, Wisconsin.

Mother's boy

Wright was quite a private child, but he was friendly with a bright, lame boy named Robie Lamp. Out of school, they designed an iceboat together and set up a 'publishing house' with its own printing press.

Even if Wright learned little in school, his mother made sure he made up for it at home. It never crossed her mind that this shy child of hers might not be a genius. She agreed with the educational theories of Friedrich Froebel, who believed that all children were capable of being creative and productive if encouraged in the right ways. So, she bought Wright some 'Froebel blocks' – cubes, spheres and cylinders of clean-cut maple wood, which could be fitted together into satisfying constructions. With these blocks, which were meant to make young children aware of colour and **form**, Wright delightedly made his very first designs. 'Those blocks stayed in my fingers all my life,' he later said.

His mother also encouraged Wright to become familiar with the natural world. He had a quiet place in the house to draw and keep his treasure of interestingly shaped stones. Wright read avidly, soon devouring adult books like Victor Hugo's *Hunchback of Notre Dame*, which contained a chapter on architecture that caught his fancy. This pleased his mother because, according to Wright's *Autobiography*, she had decided before his birth how he should show his brilliance: 'The boy, she said, was to build beautiful buildings… she intended him to be an architect.'

There is no record of what Wright's father had in mind for him. In 1884 his views ceased to matter when the marriage finally broke down. Wright Senior moved out and asked for a divorce, which he got in 1885. It is unlikely that Wright ever saw his father again. Nor did he attend his funeral at Lone Rock in 1904. From 1884, his only true family was the Lloyd Jones clan. According to his mother, his father had left her with just one 50-cent piece. Now Wright, as head of the household, had to make sure that the family did not sink into total poverty.

FIRST STEPS TOWARDS FAME

Wright had his mother to thank for his first paid work. She pulled some strings to get him a part-time job as a **draftsman** with Allan D. Conover, a **civil engineer** at the University of Wisconsin. In the mornings he also studied civil engineering at the university. He enjoyed this grounding in both the principles and practice of construction work, while reading hungrily about art and architecture in his spare time. In 1886 he assisted architect Joseph Lyman Silsbee in the drafting and building of Unity Chapel, the Lloyd Jones family chapel near Spring Green. But even at this early stage, Wright had itchy feet. In 1887, at the age of 20, he decided to leave behind small-town America and move to a great **metropolis**: Chicago.

Wright in the 'Windy City'

Wright arrived in the city of Chicago in Illinois on a drizzly night in 1887. He worked for a year as a draftsman for J.L. Silsbee. This gave him a sound knowledge of how to design houses. Then the architectural firm of Adler and Sullivan took him on.

Louis Sullivan, one of the great architects of the time, took Wright under his wing. He saw that the younger man was keen, efficient

Chicago

By the mid- to late 19th century, Chicago had become a great commercial city with around a million inhabitants. It was ideally situated for commerce, positioned in the middle of America between the manufacturing east and the farming west, and was connected to all other parts by road, rail, river and lake. Many buildings were made of wood, so when a fire started in a barn on the outskirts of the city in October 1871, it spread rapidly, fanned by the abundant winds blowing from the **prairies**. The Great Fire decimated the city: 18,000 buildings in an area of 6.5 km^2 were razed to the ground. But because of its prime position Chicago was quickly rebuilt.

and already an exceptionally good designer. 'He loved to talk to me,' Wright later wrote in his *Autobiography*, 'and I would often stay listening, after dark, in the offices in the upper stories of the great tower of the Auditorium building looking out over Lake Michigan, or over the lighted city.'

The architect Louis Sullivan, of the Chicago firm Adler and Sullivan. Wright never forgot how much he learned from his *'Lieber Meister'* – beloved master. In 1949 Wright published *Genius and the Mobocracy*, a biography of Sullivan.

Sullivan had made his name designing new buildings for Chicago after the Great Fire in 1871. He made his architectural ideals widely known through his writings. These included a belief that architecture ought to express the spirit of the function of a building. So a waterworks, for example, should not simply function as an efficient pumping machine. Its design should also, somehow, give an impression of flowing water. He coined a famous phrase, '**Form** follows function', which impressed Wright greatly. He also believed strongly that buildings in the USA should have a distinctly modern American style, and not an old-fashioned or European feel.

Wright worked for Sullivan for six years, steadily increasing his responsibilities. Although his salary also increased, Wright was spending more and more as he had inherited his father's inability to handle money carefully. He was running up serious debts by playing as hard as he worked – he had conquered his youthful shyness in an exciting round of parties, concerts and theatre visits.

13

Catherine L. Wright was a beauty who came very close to Wright's youthful ideal of an 'intimate fairy princess', who would inspire him to great deeds and 'unquenchable triumphs'.

Becoming a family man

Soon after arriving in Chicago, Wright met someone else who would have a profound influence on his life. Catherine Lee Tobin, usually known as Kitty, was sixteen when she first met Wright. They married two years later, on 1 June 1889, when Wright was almost 22. She came from a prosperous Chicago family, had a fine sense of humour and was devoted to her talented and industrious husband, on occasion even wearing clothes that he had designed.

She could be very strong-minded too; a popular saying in the Tobin family was, 'Often in error, but seldom in doubt!' One of her nieces said of Kitty, 'She talked faster than she listened.'

"
Wright's son David recalled in later life, 'As a family we got along very well, but we were all opinionated and hard on each other. [There were] a lot of criticisms. But we were united against the outside world. Fights? Oh, yes, there were plenty of those. I remember after Dad put us in the dormitory, there was a seven-foot partition dividing the girls' side from the boys', and when our sisters were having slumber parties we would throw a pillow over the partition. It took some skill.'
"

But Kitty failed to impress Wright's mother Anna, who lived next door for much of their marriage. Anna never found it easy to share her beloved son with another woman. She advised him not to marry Kitty, then fainted at the wedding, and went on to make her new daughter-in-law's life difficult in numerous small ways. Meanwhile she acquired a gaggle of grandchildren. First there was Lloyd (1890–1978), then John (1892–1972), followed by Catherine (1894–1979), David (1895–1997), Frances (1898–1959) and Llewellyn (1903–86).

Oak Park – an early masterpiece

In 1889, with the help of a generous loan from Sullivan, Wright designed a house that was built in Oak Park, a suburb 16 kilometres (10 miles) to the west of Chicago. It still stands today, and is a fine example of Wright's early architectural principles. From the outside it looked quiet and simple, combining dark stained **shingles** and brick terrace walls with white stone **coping**. Inside, it was originally full of

Oak Park, Illinois – the home that Wright built for himself in 1889.

oriental rugs, Japanese prints, bowls of wildflowers and busts of Beethoven. Later he made the interior far less cluttered, so that the rooms flowed into one another even more smoothly. He also left the wood in its natural state, and did not cover the plaster with wallpaper or bright, shiny paint.

The heart of the house was its fireplace. Families gathered before the hearths in their homes, and Wright believed that the family unit was an almost sacred thing. So, from the beginning, fireplaces often figured strongly in the houses he designed. The one at Oak Park stood in its own private nook, and over the fireplace two inscriptions were carved into a smooth, wooden panel. One said: *Truth is Life*. The other said: *Good Friend, Around These Hearth-Stones Speak No Evil Of Any Creature.*

The playroom at Oak Park which was added in 1895. Wright designed the large mural over the fireplace based on a tale from *The Arabian Nights*. He later described it as, 'First straight line ornament. FLLW designer.'

'A jolly carnival'

Wright lived in the Oak Park house for 20 years, during which time the building was transformed again and again. Ever restless, Wright made changes on average every six months. One major change came in 1898 when he built a studio next door, complete with some of his own stained-glass window designs. This was now to be his regular place of work. But despite the changes, he always preserved the house's sense of proportion. He liked to say that he made all his houses fit a 'normal-sized' person. This, naturally, meant a person who was 174 centimetres tall – just like himself!

He worked phenomenally hard during his years at Oak Park, putting down his ideas very fast, often in finished form. In old age, he would say that he 'rolled ideas out of his sleeve'. He liked to draw plans late at night or close to dawn, when the children were asleep. He loved to be confronted in his drawing-office by a blank sheet of paper under a direct white light. There he would set to work with his freshly sharpened coloured pencils. Kitty might heighten his creative mood by playing Bach or by preparing his favourite meal – freshly baked onions. A servant would keep his fire going in winter, or bring in supplies of iced lemonade during the hot months.

Although Wright's children saw little of their father, there were still memorable musical evenings for all the family. Wright had a knack for cheering up anyone who became downcast. 'Papa would roguishly laugh them out of it,' his son John remembered. 'He was an epic of wit and merriment that gave our home the feeling of a jolly carnival.'

When a burglar broke into Oak Park (the doors were never locked because Wright did not like to carry keys), Wright heard the break-in, and turned on the lights so that the thief could see what he was burgling. Instead of becoming furious or afraid, he asked the intruder why 'so handsome a fellow didn't get out and work in the light where he could be seen and appreciated!' The burglar's reply is not recorded.

'EYE MUSIC'

In 1893 Wright left Adler and Sullivan, after Sullivan discovered that Wright had been accepting **commissions** without the company's knowledge. He set up his own architectural **practice** from Oak Park, working there until 1909. Wright prepared a full set of **working drawings** every six weeks on average – usually for wealthy professional clients – and a large proportion of his designs ended up as actual buildings, unlike those of many other architects. Wright had a very exact vision of how the buildings should look; he took control over the fine details of both the interiors and the exteriors. It was clear to all who saw his buildings that he was paying little heed to past architectural traditions in realizing his architectural vision.

A brand new American style

Wright's first independent commission at 26 years of age turned out to be a triumph. This was the elegant house he designed for William H. Winslow in River Forest, Illinois. It still draws the highest praise from critics today. In his book *Frank Lloyd Wright: Master Builder*, the author B.B. Pfeiffer says that it 'marks the beginning of a new language in domestic architecture for the United States'. Built from the simple, natural materials of Roman brick, cast concrete and **terracotta**, it was moulded together in a brand new style that suited the American environment and paid little tribute to European models. This was one of Wright's earliest attempts to create a natural link between humankind and its environment. Later he would refer to this aspect of his work as '**organic** architecture', taking into account the needs of the client, the nature of the site and whatever native materials were available.

From the outside, the house looked very 'modern' alongside the grand, high-peaked turrets of the neighbouring houses, which were typical of the late **Victorian** period. Its sleek, uncluttered interior was also different. Wright wanted the house to create a sense of freedom, rather than follow strict **classical** rules. He referred to this sense of freedom as '**plasticity**', or 'continuity in the building itself'. 'Have no

Wright's Winslow House of 1893, built at River Forest, Illinois. Its external differences from most other late Victorian houses (bottom) are clear to see. Internally it was far more 'modern', too.

beams, no columns, no cornices, nor any fixtures, nor **pilasters** or **entablatures** as such,' he once wrote. 'Instead of two things, one thing. Let walls, ceilings, floors become part of each, growing into one another, getting continuity out of it all or into it all, eliminating any constructed feature.'

The prairie house years

For Adler and Sullivan, Wright had specialized in domestic architecture – that is, residential homes, rather than commercial projects, like opera houses or concert halls. In later years, he would win international acclaim for buildings like a great hotel in Tokyo (see page 29) and a great museum in New York (see pages 48–50). But at the turn of the century he made his name in domestic design. And some people still believe that Wright's houses from the early 1900s were his most original and important contributions to the **evolution** of architecture.

More than 20 of these '**prairie** houses', or houses built in the 'prairie style', still stand in and around Oak Park. Some other Chicago architects worked along similar lines, but Wright was the best-known practitioner of the style. 'I loved the prairie,' he wrote. 'The trees, flowers and sky were thrilling by contrast… a little height on the prairie was enough to look like much more. Notice how every detail as to height becomes intensely significant and how breadths all fall short.' To suit such an environment, he believed that people's houses should have long, low, graceful lines, without attics or basements: 'I began to see a building primarily not as a cave, but as broad shelter in the open, related to **vista**; vista without and vista within.'

The Ward W. Willits house built in 1902 at Highland Park, Illinois, is typical of Wright's prairie style. Built using cement **stucco** and elegant wood trim, Wright described the house's visual effect, both external and internal, as 'eye music'.

Wright did not design all his prairie houses to a formula. He made each building fit in with its own particular setting, as well as with each client's particular needs. But his aim was always to abolish the sense of the house being a 'box'. This meant letting the rooms flow into one another by eliminating unnecessary walls and doors, and allowing the dwelling to open out on to the landscape. He also rejected the idea of treating windows as individual holes cut into walls. Instead, on both the upper and lower **storeys**, he grouped them together as long, continuous bands of light.

Wright in about 1905. As his fame grew, he never suffered from false modesty. 'Early in life,' he wrote, 'I had to choose between honest arrogance and hypocritical humility. I chose honest arrogance.'

Houses on a human scale

Both inside and out, Wright wanted his prairie houses to exhibit the 'American' qualities of honesty, simplicity and frankness. This can be seen in the austere, yet elegant, furniture in the picture on page 20. Few can now deny that the prairie house was a new type of dwelling – both practical and beautiful. But not everyone shared his lack of respect for the classical architectural traditions of Europe, and his early work received a lot of criticism.

Since the late 1700s, house design had often been a formal architectural exercise, requiring strict adherence to established rules and proportions. Houses were still regarded primarily as monuments and symbols of status at the turn of the 20th century. It was only under the influences of Ruskin and Morris (see box below) that architects started to design houses as homes. Wright, like other major architects of the early 1900s, was mainly concerned with the dwellings of ordinary people – albeit those sufficiently well-off to employ him.

And, unlike many architects, Wright was notable for quantity as well as quality. The **Frank Lloyd Wright Foundation** has listed more than

Old World influences on a New World master builder

In 1880s Britain, under the leadership of William Morris, the Arts and Crafts Movement became highly influential. It was a reaction to the mass production introduced by the **Industrial Revolution**, and sought to revive the tradition of handcrafted objects of lasting beauty and utility. As a younger man, Wright was deeply impressed by the principles of this Movement. He was also inspired by the writings of English art critic John Ruskin, who had first coined the phrase 'organic architecture'. According to Ruskin, architecture had an obligation to improve society, and beauty existed in order 'to convey the absolute values upon which a sound society must rest'. The Arts and Crafts Movement, like Ruskin and Wright after him, set great store by translating high ideals into bricks and mortar. And Wright was especially keen on its principle that every aspect of a design, from the chimney trim to the place mats, should be part of a grand 'unified' concept.

While Wight admired the ancient building styles of – among others – the Etruscans, Chinese, Egyptians and Persians, he argued that, 'it would only be an idiot who would try to bring it home and plant it under different conditions to which it did not belong'.

150 buildings designed by Wright that were actually constructed during this fertile first period of his career.

As his fame grew in the early 1900s, so did Wright's appreciation of his own talents. His tastes became more expensive and showy – from a more flamboyant dress sense (a flaring cape or a completely unnecessary cane) to fast cars and horses – although he did not always have enough money to afford them.

In Unity Temple, built in 1905, Wright considered the convenience of the worshippers when he inventively built 'a temple to man' out of poured concrete with integrated heating.

FAMILY FERMENT

" 'Frank Lloyd Wright placed great faith in the family unit as the essential core of a free **democracy**. His mission was to create an architectural environment that would address the individual and the family unit first of all, and then society as a whole.' From *Frank Lloyd Wright: Master Builder* by B.B. Pfeiffer (1997). "

Wright had come to fame as a family man. He came from a large, close-knit family himself, then with Kitty he fathered six children of his own. But by 1909 something was going wrong within this second family unit, just as something had gone badly wrong in the first.

'The absorbing, consuming phase of my experience as an architect ended about 1909,' he later wrote. 'I had almost reached my fortieth year: weary, I was losing grip on my work and even interest in it... I could see no way out. Because I did not know what I wanted, I wanted to go away... Everything, personal or otherwise, bore down heavily on me. Domesticity most of all. What I wanted I did not know. I loved my children. I loved my home. A true home is the finest ideal of man...' But by his fortieth year, Wright's own true home was no longer Oak Park. In 1909 he left both his family and his flourishing architectural **practice** to travel to Europe – with another woman.

This is the only known photo of Mamah Borthwick Cheney, the married woman Wright turned to between 1909 and 1914, after he lost his belief in his own marriage.

'A house divided'

The woman was Mamah Borthwick Cheney, the pretty and clever wife of a client for whom Wright had built a house in 1904. No one – including Wright himself – could be sure what led him to destroy so much of what he believed in. He claimed that Kitty had become far more interested in the children than in him, and that they had married when they were too young. In a letter to his mother he said that he was 'a house divided against itself by circumstances I can not control'.

His behaviour scandalized the 'respectable' people of Chicago (and the number of **commissions** from them fell sharply as a result). But Wright was not the kind of man to admit he had done something wrong. 'The ordinary man cannot live without rules to guide his life,' he wrote. 'It is infinitely more difficult to live without rules, but that is what the really honest, sincere, thinking man is compelled to do. And I think when a man has displayed some spiritual power, has given concrete evidence of his ability to see and feel the higher and better things of life, we ought to go slow in deciding he has acted badly.'

Kitty's tolerance was severely strained, yet she kept hoping that, after his return from Europe in 1910, Wright would come back to her and the children at Oak Park – even though his passion for Mamah showed no sign of fizzling out. In 1912 Kitty confidently predicted to a friend that the affair would be over in two years' time. She was to be proved right in a most gruesome fashion.

Radiant brow

Wright's time in Europe was spent usefully as well as enjoyably. While there, he worked on a **portfolio** of his work that was published by Ernst Wasmuth. The 'Wasmuth Portfolio' brought him far wider international recognition, and greatly inspired other architects. Meanwhile in Fiesole, Italy, Wright was himself inspired by seeing the Villa Medici, a lovely country house on a Tuscan hillside. Even before returning to the USA, he was sketching plans for a similar home, studio and farm to be shared by him and Mamah. Once back, the

The inspiration behind Taliesin

In *An Autobiography*, Wright described how the Villa Medici at Fiesole inspired him to build Taliesin: 'I saw the hill-crown back of the house as one mass of apple trees in bloom… I saw plum trees, fragrant drifts of snow-white in the spring… I saw thickly pendant clusters of rubies like tassels in the dark leaves of the currant bushes… I saw the vineyard… Yes, Taliesin should be a garden and a farm behind a real workshop and a good home.'

construction began in the valley where he grew up, near Spring Green, Wisconsin – adding fresh fuel to the fires of scandal. Local newspapers gleefully followed the goings-on at the bungalow they dubbed Wright's 'love nest'.

Named 'Taliesin', the finished complex of buildings was wrapped around the brow of a hill. Built from local golden-yellow limestone, and cement plaster made with sand from the Wisconsin River, with low

Taliesin – the focal point of Wright's life in the years after he moved out of his Oak Park family home. The name was Welsh and meant 'radiant brow'.

spreading roofs of cedar **shingles**, it overlooked water gardens created by damming a nearby stream. The interior was finished in cypress wood, with floors paved in limestone flagstone or wide boards of waxed cypress, and with art objects blending quietly into the soft, serene atmosphere. But Taliesin was far more than just a home – Wright's studio, drafting room and office were next to the living quarters. Further courts and levels provided places for **draftsmen**, workmen and farmers to live. Cows, pigs, goats and chickens were kept in additional outbuildings – still connected by roofs and courts.

'The whole,' Wright wrote, 'was low, wide and snug, a broad shelter seeking fellowship with its surroundings… Taliesin's order was such that when all was clean and in place its **countenance** beamed, wore a happy smile of well-being and welcome for all. It was intensely human, I believe.'

Yet this intensely human haven was not destined to survive. On 15 August 1914, while Wright was away in Chicago, disaster struck. A servant, Julian Carlton, set fire to Taliesin's living quarters and went on a killing spree that ended with the deaths of seven people, including Mamah and her two children.

This was the symbol Wright designed for his architectural practice – a cross inside a circle inside a square, based on old **Celtic** British **motifs**.

NEW HORIZONS

> *'I know how to be a lover but I have never learned how to be a friend. (I feel that now I must learn.),'* wrote Wright after losing Mamah. *'And I have been so utterly flung back upon myself, dammed at flood-tide... as I hunger for the living touch of someone – something, intimately peculiar to myself – inviolably 'mine'. Yes – at times almost anyone or anything.'*

After the tragedy, Wright started to rebuild his life and Taliesin. Although the living quarters had been destroyed, the studio and a small bedroom had survived. From this nucleus, Wright steadily rebuilt his great house on the hill. 'Taliesin lived wherever I stood,' he once said. But he did not plan to live there on his own. Wright's quest for a perfect relationship continued in earnest. And, before the end of 1914, amazingly, he believed he might have found it.

A new soulmate

Wright received many letters of sympathy from complete strangers after the fire. One came from Miriam Noel, a woman two years younger than Wright. She was a divorced sculptress who had once lived in Paris. Unlike Wright's other well-wishers, she then wrote a second letter, offering him helpful advice and asking if he would grant her an interview. Intrigued, Wright agreed to see her. When they met he found her beautiful and interesting, if a little highly-strung.

Miriam Noel, who came into Wright's life in 1914 and finally married him in 1923.

Wright's Imperial Hotel, Tokyo, was not universally acclaimed: 'Fascinating, ingenious and unique are the words that leap to mind... probably equally applicable to a rabbit warren,' said one critic.

She appealed to him particularly because she told him she knew how painful it was to lose a loved one. But within a very short time they became long-term lovers themselves. It was a passionate, sometimes tempestuous relationship. 'Lord of my Waking Dreams!' Miriam called Wright. There was no danger of her – unlike Kitty – failing to give him her full and undivided adulation. But Kitty still hoped against hope that he would return to her. Partly for that reason she continued to refuse him a divorce.

So, until 1923, Wright and Miriam had to live together 'in sin' – that is, without being married. This did nothing to improve Wright's reputation for 'immorality' in the USA, but for much of that time they lived not in the American Midwest, but in Tokyo, Japan.

To Tokyo

From 1916 to 1922, most of Wright's professional energies went into designing the Imperial Hotel in Tokyo. Wright had been fascinated by oriental art, architecture and culture since his first visit to Japan in 1905. He had amassed a great collection of Japanese prints, many of

29

which adorned Taliesin. So he was especially honoured to receive the **commission** to design such a prestigious building in the Japanese capital. The completed hotel would, he believed, confirm his stature as an architect of truly global significance.

The construction was not trouble-free, however. There was a language barrier between Wright, assisted now by his son John, and the Japanese engineers and workmen. And, as with many of Wright's works in progress, costs soared – the owners finally calculated that they had to pay three times the original estimate. But by 4 July 1922 the first guests were staying in Wright's broad-winged, lion-coloured structure of lava, concrete and brick.

Wright had made the 'Impeho' look impressive – both inside and out – but it also had to stand up to Tokyo's intermittent earthquakes. To this end 'Wrieto-San' – as his Japanese colleagues called him – devised a way to absorb any shocks by sinking the central supports for the hotel into soft earth, to hold up the floor slabs 'as a waiter balances a tray on his fingers'. It was an unusual method of underpinning, and even Wright must have had occasional doubts about how successfully it would cope with actual tremors.

Californian interlude

At the same time as working on the Imperial Hotel, Wright and Miriam made several trips back to the USA. Commissions in his native Midwest were drying up, but his designs were in greater demand in California. Hoping to set up a permanent **practice** there, he took on several major assignments, the most important of which was a distinctive Los Angeles home for oil heiress Aline Barnsdall. Wright's attention to detail was as thorough as ever – because the hollyhock was Barnsdall's favourite flower, he built **abstractions** of the plant into the decoration.

When the Tokyo project was finished, Wright and Miriam settled briefly in Los Angeles, where Wright opened an office, before returning to Taliesin. The couple's roller-coaster relationship showed no signs of becoming smoother, but in 1922 Kitty finally gave Wright his divorce, and in the following year he married Miriam. In between times, two

large events occurred. First, Wright's mother died and was buried in the cemetery of Unity Chapel. She had lived to see her beloved son surpass even her own dreams for him as an architect, but she had found Miriam no more acceptable than Kitty as a partner for him. Secondly, a catastrophic earthquake struck Tokyo.

About 140,000 people lost their lives as buildings toppled all round. Communication with the outside world was lost, and rumours reached American newspapers that the Imperial Hotel was in ruins. 'Frank was so wounded [by this news],' Miriam wrote, 'I thought he would die that week.' But later the truth emerged. The hotel, only slightly damaged, had been used as a home for refugees and also as a temporary base for embassies and the press. Wright's reputation had remained intact.

> " This telegram brought Wright the news from Tokyo in September 1923: 'Hotel stands undamaged as monument of your genius. Hundreds of homeless provided [for] by perfectly maintained service. Congratulations.' "

'THE RADICAL CONSERVATIVE'

Wright and his second wife lived together for barely six months. In May 1924 Miriam moved out and left him. The love between them seemed to have vanished completely. Over the next four years they wrangled bitterly over the divorce **settlement** she was to receive, and inevitably the media gave a good deal of attention to their disputes. Wright believed her to be quite insane by now – destabilized by the various medications she used. But he had problems in his professional as well as his personal life.

A man out of his time?

After his dizzying triumphs in Japan and California, Wright came back to earth with a bump on his return to Taliesin. He still saw himself as a pioneer for **quintessentially** American architecture. But to many he now seemed like yesterday's man, and fewer and fewer clients **commissioned** his designs. The worlds of art and architecture had changed greatly in the years since World War I (see box below) and whereas Wright had once cut a revolutionary figure, now he could seem almost traditional.

Norris Kelly Smith in his 1966 book, *Frank Lloyd Wright: a Study in Architectural Content*, described Wright's new position in this way: 'He

---

A new wave in the arts

In the early 20th century, artistic movements with names such as Futurism, Fauvism and Dadaism gave rise to new approaches in architecture, too. Leading European architects of the 'International Style', like Le Corbusier, Gropius and Mies van der Rohe, tried to adapt their work to the demands of the new machine age and mass production. They designed boxy, uniform buildings that were little more than 'machines for living'. The **aesthetic** of beauty, which meant so much to Wright, had little place in their work. And his belief in creative fantasy now seemed self-indulgent to many.

prided himself upon being a revolutionary trail blazer, responsible for the principal innovations that have determined the character of all modern architecture, but at the same time he regarded himself as the defender of a universal **organic** ideal whose nature has been misunderstood by virtually all modern architects.' One phrase that Wright sometimes applied to himself was '**radical** conservative' – that is, someone who worked in the classic architectural tradition of **evolutionary** change. Even so, in the mid- to late 1920s, with his insistence on beauty and individuality, he seemed to be an outsider, increasingly out of step with the times.

In a world where houses like this one – designed by Le Corbusier – were the 'New Look', Wright's own designs seemed no longer to be at the cutting edge of architecture.

Yet Wright had grown up with the family motto, 'Truth against the World'. He relished challenges of all kinds – especially when he had a female ally at his side. And in 1924 he met his most enduring ally of all – Olgivanna Lazovich.

This remarkable woman had, according to the author Daniel Treiber, 'a personality sufficiently similar to Wright's own to be accepted, but strong enough not to be crushed'. Wright would need the support of Olgivanna so he could continue to work during the difficulties of the coming **Depression**.

Wright with Olgivanna Lazovich, his third wife, with whom he had a daughter, Iovanna, in 1925. Olgivanna already had a daughter, Svetlana, from a previous marriage.

The third Mrs Wright

Wright's turbulent relationship with Miriam began with a fire at Taliesin. By a strange coincidence, once the relationship was over, a second fire half destroyed his showpiece home in 1925. Again, Wright began to rebuild immediately, and again, he had someone beside him with whom he planned to share it.

Wright met Olga Iovanna Lazovich at a ballet performance in Chicago in 1924. ('Olgivanna' came from running her first two names together.) More than 30 years younger than Wright (who was now 57), she came from Montenegro in the European **Balkans**. With one failed marriage behind her, and a young daughter named Svetlana, she had left her wealthy family to follow Georgei Ivanovich Gurdjieff – a mysterious teacher who had constructed his own philosophy of spiritual development. His methods ranged from exercise, dance and strenuous physical labour to psychological disciplines that were supposed to awaken his followers from 'the profound slumber of humankind'. Gurdjieff and his teachings captivated the beautiful Olgivanna – later she wrote *The Struggle Within* (1955) which paid tribute to his great influence. Now, in Wright, she found a man of similar charisma. But instead of becoming his disciple, she married him, had his child, Iovanna, and remained his invaluable partner at Taliesin for over 30 years until his death.

Olgivanna (left foreground) with other followers of Gurdjieff. At his command, they all had to stop whatever they were doing, and so wake from the 'sleep' of their daily grind.

Frank Lloyd Wrong?

Despite having found true love, the late 1920s were hard times for Wright. The second Taliesin fire set him back by $200,000. That was a huge sum for a man who seldom seemed **solvent** even when – unlike now – work commissions were flooding in. Then there was the matter of satisfying Miriam over their divorce settlement. This was a bitter and costly business, finalized only in 1927 (and followed in 1928 by Wright's marriage to Olgivanna at Santa Fe in California). Wright was so deeply in debt that a group of his friends devised a way to finance him through this lean spell.

It seemed absurd to them that so famous a figure should go bankrupt – it was already hard enough for him to be known locally as Frank Lloyd Wrong, on account of his 'immorality', and to be regarded only as a Past Master as an architect. Wright's friends and clients set him afloat again financially by 'incorporating' him. This meant, in effect, that the great architect was turned into a **stock company**, with his supporters buying shares in him. The funds thus raised were used to pay off his debts – on the understanding that Wright would repay his investors out of his future earnings. But as the Depression deepened, Wright knew that he could not rely on commissions alone to raise cash. Then he hit upon the idea of the Fellowship.

The new Taliesin community

In August 1932 Wright announced the Taliesin Fellowship. He had always had young associates around him in his work, but now he began a career as their paid educator. Trainees would work for him as apprentices in residence, helping to restore the buildings, while learning 'essential architecture' against a background of 'Philosophy, Sculpture, Painting, Music and the Industrial Crafts'. His aim was not just to train up good architects, but to produce responsible, creative and cultured human beings.

The ambitious programme was run as much by Olgivanna as by Wright. To keep it running smoothly, she drew from her experiences as a member of Gurdjieff's community, while Wright sought to create an atmosphere similar to that in his own family when he was younger.

The Fellowship commenced on 1 October 1932. All 23 places were filled immediately. Each apprentice had to pay an annual fee of $650, and in the following years young people came from all over the globe. Most of them were so thrilled to learn from 'Mr Wright' that they gladly did the domestic donkey work expected of them at Taliesin. Although Olgivanna once claimed that 'servants were vulgar, and had no place

Princeton principles

In a 1930s lecture at Princeton University, Wright set out his main principles as a designer of houses. They included:

- reducing the separate rooms to a minimum, and making all come together as enclosed space
- associating the building as a whole with its site
- eliminating the room as a box and the house as another
- using no ornament that did not come out of the nature of the materials
- incorporating the furnishings as organic architecture, making them fully integrated with the building and designing them in simple terms so that they could be made by machines.

Wright with Fellowship apprentices at Taliesin in 1938, who were 'maybe in the kitchen one day, and the next day driving a tractor… but nearly every day… in the drawing-office making plans…'

at Taliesin,' some observers felt that the apprentices were treated as servants – and they had to pay their master for this privilege!

Although he was now over 60 years old, Wright still pushed himself very hard. Always an early riser, he often started work hours before breakfast. He claimed that his best ideas came to him out on the farm, in the fields and woods or beside the stream. 'Many times he came to the studio direct from the farm,' wrote one of his **draftsmen**, 'refreshed and bursting to put new ideas on paper.' At other times he came in clutching an envelope, on which he had scribbled down a design solution that came to him in the middle of the night.

He then worked at his drafting board with immense patience and concentration. Fanatical about detail, he went through countless revisions until he felt sure he had captured the 'soul' of a projected new building. He could put any personal troubles out of his mind when he worked and always entered his studio a happy man. Now and then he would relax by playing Bach or Beethoven on his piano, or lovingly admire a new set of Japanese prints.

But ideas were one thing and clients were another. Some clients could be very demanding indeed, and Wright had to be flexible enough to adapt his designs to suit them – or politely persuade them to change their minds. Yet according to an employee, 'He had the highest regard for each of his clients simply because they were his clients; he found virtues in them which were **indiscernible** to others and almost refused to acknowledge their shortcomings.' And, as the 1930s wore on, there were more and more clients to deal with. For his career now took a startling turn for the better, even though the fortunes of his beloved USA had taken a severe turn for the worse...

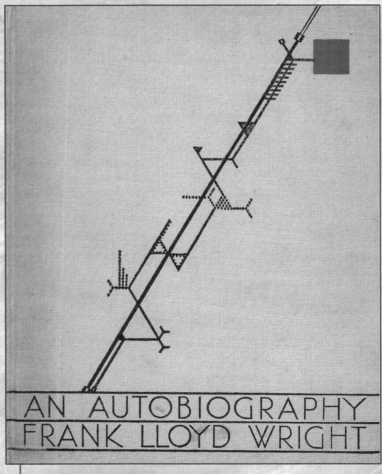

AN AUTOBIOGRAPHY
FRANK LLOYD WRIGHT

In 1932, Wright published his *Autobiography*, dedicated 'To my co-author Olgivanna from her own "author" Frank Lloyd Wright.' He turned increasingly to writing and lecturing in an attempt to make ends meet.

Wright's response to adversity

The great financial crisis of 1929 and the Depression that followed it had a huge economic impact on all Americans. Wright responded by putting much of his imaginative effort into providing affordable housing for the average American family, and also into **decentralized** planning to relieve crowded cities.

His solutions were the 'Usonian' house and 'Broadacre City'. Usonian was a word based on the letters of USA, and described the kind of architecture that Wright proposed for all over America. His vision included new, cheap methods of house construction, as well as changes in the concept of the residential plan. His main objective was to simplify all aspects of construction, eliminating everything unnecessary – from features to materials.

Wright's 1933 house for Malcolm Willey in Minneapolis put these idealistic principles into practice. And, during the 1930s, Wright's clients did tend to come from less wealthy ranks of society than before. The Broadacre City project (see below) was born at Taliesin at a time when hardly any commissions were coming into the office. Wright assigned the apprentices of the Taliesin Fellowship to assist him in designing this idealistic model, which was finally exhibited across the USA.

Broadacre City

In the words of B.B. Pfeiffer, Broadacre City implemented Wright's ideas about decentralization, 'moving the vital components of the overcrowded city into the healthy environment of the country and redesigning the architecture required by such a Usonian community so that the buildings would enhance the life of its citizens and also become integral features of the natural landscape.' It got its name from Wright's idea that the city should be spread out, so that each householder could live on an acre of land on which most of the family's food could be grown.

THE GREAT TURNAROUND

'Wright's surge of creativity after two decades of frustration,' wrote Robert Twombly in his 1973 biography of the architect, 'was one of the great **resuscitations** in American art history, made more impressive by the fact that Wright was 70 years old in 1937.' Frank Lloyd Wright never quite lost his self-belief and conviction that some of his finest work was still to be done. Everyone who thought he was history could now only gape in wonder as his career enjoyed a splendid late flowering.

From 1932 until Wright's death in 1959, the Fellowship made it possible for Wright to produce a great deal of work – if required. His production team was a core group of half a dozen permanent Fellowship members. They helped to train new apprentices, to complete studio drafting work, and to represent Wright at various sites around the country. As it happened, there was a sudden upsurge in **commissions**. Partly this was because Wright's designs again synchronized with fashion. Partly it was inspired by two great buildings of his from the mid-1930s – buildings which still rank among his all-time masterpieces.

The house in the waterfall

If a single building restored Wright's reputation, it was the home he designed for Edgar J. Kaufmann at Bear Run, Pennsylvania in 1935. Fallingwater, as it was called, deserved its name. For this cliffside construction sat immediately above a waterfall, a favourite leisure spot of the Kaufmann family (a son of which had been an apprentice at Taliesin). Wright wanted the Kaufmanns 'not simply to look at the waterfalls but to live with them'. The resulting dwelling represented perhaps his most harmonious match between man and nature (see also picture page 5).

The house was anchored into the cliff ledges and had three levels, each with its own terrace, with outside stairways leading to further terraces. It was a fantasy of reinforced concrete, local stone, expansive glass windows and French doors – the whole concept suggested by the

At Fallingwater, wrote Wright, 'nature and art were made to complement one another.' Even the windows at the far end of the living room offered 'structured **vistas**' of the gorgeous scenery outside, like a series of paintings.

immediate environment. Wright even incorporated into his design a large boulder where the family had once sunbathed; now it became the hearthstone for the fireplace.

Fallingwater has been called 'the most significant residence built in the United States'. Soaring in all directions, it seems to defy gravity. And its breathtaking **cantilevers**, echoing branches in the surrounding trees, defy modern ideas about safety, too. In 1992 a structural engineer remarked that 'there is not a city in the United States, even today some 57 years later, where one could obtain a building permit to erect Fallingwater'. But out in the remote Pennsylvania countryside in the mid-1930s, Wright got away with it. He was justly proud of his achievement — and it may be no accident that his favourite way of signing his own initials crops up in the name of this landmark triumph in his long career: FaLLingWater.

Wright in conversation with Edgar J. Kaufmann Snr., who commissioned Fallingwater. They are sitting in Wright's 'desert camp' – Taliesin West, in Arizona – where he escaped each harsh Wisconsin winter.

The desert camp

Wright's second masterpiece of the 1930s was built in the western desertland of Arizona. Wright had first spent time there in 1927, as a consultant for the Arizona Biltmore Hotel. Then in 1934–35 he brought part of the Fellowship there to work on his models for Broadacre City (see page 39). He became so attached to the region, that he decided to build a headquarters there for the winters.

The new home and workshop – Taliesin West – was camp-like at first and intended only for winter use. But as Wright returned each season with his family and apprentices, he planned for the buildings to

> "
> *'I was struck by the beauty of the desert, by the dry, clear sun-drenched air, by the stark geometry of the mountains – the entire region was an inspiration in strong contrast to the lush, pastoral landscape of my native Wisconsin. And out of that experience, a revelation is what I guess you might call it, came the design for these buildings. The design sprang out of itself, with no precedent and nothing following it.'*
> "
> Wright on the creation of Taliesin West.

become more permanent. Based on desert stones of richly varied colours that were set into concrete made with local sand, a magnificent structure evolved. Its massive walls reared up at odd sloping angles, reflecting the slopes of the nearby mountain ranges. A network of redwood **trusses** was set on these walls, and in between them were frames with stretched white canvas, which let in some of Arizona's 'dry, clear sun-drenched air' which so appealed to Wright.

Like the reconstructed Taliesin in Wisconsin, Taliesin West was built mostly by the Fellowship apprentices. At first, electricity came from a diesel generator, and water from a self-drilled well. It was like a magical oasis inside its enclosing walls, while outside the desert landscape stayed entirely untouched. As Wright once wrote: 'when **organic** architecture is properly carried out no landscape is ever outraged by it, but is always developed by it. The good building makes the landscape more beautiful.'

'It is indeed ironic,' commented B.B. Pfeiffer, author and former apprentice of Wright's, 'that America's greatest architect would live in two homes built by young men and women in the act of learning the art of architecture.'

The pavilion at the extraordinary Taliesin West – built and maintained by apprentices, most of whom were construction novices. For over 20 years it served as Wright's architectural laboratory. It was here that Wright tested design innovations, structural ideas and building details.

'A NATIONAL LIVING TREASURE'

When World War II broke out in 1939, Wright was 72 years old. He was in the public eye again; he featured on the cover of *Time* magazine in 1938, and in the same year a whole issue of *Architectural Forum* was dedicated to his work. Even so, not even Wright could have guessed that he had two more successful decades ahead of him.

Johnson Wax Administration Building

This is the interior of the administration building that Wright completed in 1939 for S.C. Johnson and Son, makers of wax products in Racine, Wisconsin. He planned to support the main workroom's skylighted roof with 7-metre concrete columns shaped like water-lily pads with slender stems. The building licence authorities doubted that each one could support its calculated load of 6 tons each. Wright decided to stage a public test on a sample column. In front of huge crowds, he directed a crane to drop ton after ton of scrap metal onto it. In the end it gave way and crumpled – under a weight of 60 tons! When the building was opened, 30,000 people went through it in the first two days. There they enjoyed other

features like chairs that gently urged the sitter out of the seat with their inwardly leaning hinged backs, and a round birdcage lift from which passengers could survey the main floor as they ascended.

An almost humble hero

A glance at the Timeline on pages 56–59 shows how prolifically busy Wright was in the 1940s, and how much acclaim he received. Medals, **honorary doctorates**, titles and **citations** rained down on him. His private life was no longer of more interest to people than his professional output. His huge body of work (and frank opinions about other architects) made him the most prominent architect in the USA – 'a national living treasure'. But how did this great change of fortune affect the man himself? Wright said, 'somehow I expected each honour would add a certain lustre, a certain brightness to the psyche which is mine. On the contrary... it casts a shadow on my native arrogance, and for a moment I feel coming on that disease which is recommended so highly, of humility.'

However, an incident from 1937 shows the great man in his truer colours. When greater fortune came his way, Wright built up an impressive stable of vehicles in which to travel between the two Taliesins. When the first Lincoln Continental cars came onto the market, Wright took his secretary Gene Masselink and an assistant to a dealership in Chicago. The assistant later recorded: 'Mr Wright went up to the new Lincoln, tapped the fender with his stick and said, "I want one of these and one of these. Gene, show him the colour we want, the Cherokee Red." The salesman explained that the colour would have to be specially ordered. "And," Wright continued, "I want a convertible top. Take that thing off. I will send you my own design" – something like a rolltop desk. Then he declared, "and I don't expect to pay for them." He turned toward the door and added, "I expect them to be ready in two weeks".'

Usonian Automatic

Not all architects' designs end up being built. Sometimes the money cannot be found, sometimes the schemes are just too ambitious. In the mid-20th century Wright made many designs, including hospitals, opera houses and universities, which were never executed. As Chicago celebrated a Frank Lloyd Wright Day, there was even a plan for 'Mile High Illinois' – a sword-like building housing 100,000 people in no

The Fountainhead (1949), directed by King Vidor, starred Gary Cooper as an individualistic and idealistic architect, not unlike Wright.

fewer than 528 **storeys**. The drawing alone was over 6 metres tall. This was ironic, as Wright had fiercely attacked the concept of the skyscraper for years!

In 1943 Ayn Rand wrote a best-selling novel, The Fountainhead, which soon became a film, starring heart-throb Gary Cooper. Few missed the parallels between the career of the architect hero and that of Frank Lloyd Wright. Wright himself saw them – commenting that the film was 'a grossly abusive caricature of my work'. As his fame grew, Wright became ever more familiar to Americans on the TV screen. With his handsome face, snowy white hair and relaxed manner, he was a natural in front of the camera.

Wright seemed destined mainly to be a 'residential architect'. Believing that the artist must always serve society, it seemed natural to him to concentrate on society's most essential unit: the home. So he persisted with his dream of providing moderate-cost, single-storey 'Usonian' homes for less wealthy Americans (see page 39). These had features like radiant heating (through hot water pipes in the cement-slab floor), prefabricated walls made of board and cheap tar paper, **open-plan** interiors and – to reflect big changes in society – carports. Then in 1954 he published a book, The Natural House, in which he described a new concept – Usonian Automatic.

This was, in effect, a do-it-yourself attempt to avoid soaring construction costs. In the 1920s, in southern California, Wright had experimented with large concrete blocks that could be used to build a house quickly. Now he produced moulds for blocks just one foot by two in size: small enough for a single person – ideally the client – to work with. Wright showed how the blocks could be used by designing an elegant home for Gerald B. Tonkens at Amberly Village, Ohio. Still standing today, its construction was supervised by Wright's apprentice and grandson, Eric Lloyd Wright.

But around 1950, the USA – or at least its building industry – was not yet ready for Usonian Automatic. Wright had to accept relative failure in this project. Harder by far to bear was one last family tragedy, which struck in 1946. On the road to Spring Green from Taliesin, Wright's pregnant stepdaughter Svetlana was killed, along with her son, in a car accident which seemed to involve no other vehicle.

In 1946 Wright was **commissioned** to design a Unitarian Meeting House in Shorewood Hills, Wisconsin. At Olgivanna's suggestion he designed the roof to represent hands held together in prayer.

SO LONG, FRANK LLOYD WRIGHT

Wright was a practising architect for 72 years. During the last sixteen of those years he designed nearly 500 projects, almost half his lifetime output. These are amazing statistics, and a testament to his phenomenal creative energy. Several international exhibitions celebrated his achievement, most notably 'Sixty Years of Living Architecture' which opened in Florence, Italy, in 1951 and concluded its run at Wright's Hollyhock House (see page 31) in 1954.

He continued to write, publish, give addresses and dream. In 1957 – his ninetieth year, when 59 new projects came into his studio – he travelled to Baghdad, Iraq, to discuss plans with the ruling Shah for an opera house and other municipal buildings. The talks came to nothing – but only because the country was turned upside down by a revolution in 1958. In that year, 31 more **commissions** came in, raising the number of ongoing projects in the studio to a breathtaking 166.

When people asked him, 'What is your greatest work?' he had always replied with a twinkle, 'The next one.' But to many, his greatest work of all was his last one: the vast project which ran from 1943 until six months after his own death on 9 April 1959 – the museum he designed in New York City for Solomon R. Guggenheim.

The distinctive Grand Old Man of American Architecture in 1956. Always vain, he generally avoided photographers in later life because 'they all make me look like an old woman'.

> *'Here for the first time architecture appears plastic, one floor flowing into another (more like sculpture)... The whole building, cast in concrete, is more like an eggshell – in form a great simplicity – rather than like a crisscross structure. The net result of such construction is a greater **repose**, the atmosphere of the quiet unbroken wave: no meeting of the eye with abrupt changes of form. All is as one.'*
> Wright, in a book about the Guggenheim Museum, published in 1960.

'A beautiful, uninterrupted symphony'

Wright's later masterpieces such as Fallingwater (see pages 5 and 40) and the Marin County Civic Center (page 54) proved that he was an ingenious engineer as well as a genius of design. He had completely replaced the old 'boxy' concept of **post-and-beam** construction with a strong sense of the '**plastic**'. In the words of B.B. Pfeiffer, he was 'moulding buildings by means of steel and reinforced concrete, wedding engineering and architecture together in an inseparable, **organic** entity. These buildings, Wright hoped, would appear to be like flowers or trees, reflecting the concept of natural, harmonious growth "from within outward".'

His Guggenheim Museum is perhaps his most successful expression of this hope. Its astonishingly 'plastic' structure, moulded into **curvilinear form**, was cast in concrete reinforced with **filaments** of steel. As ever, the building's form was dictated by its function: to present great paintings to the public. Wright's aim was to make a single 'beautiful, uninterrupted symphony' out of both the building and the paintings on show inside it. But his design was so **radical** that he had to fight with the museum and city authorities for thirteen years before they accepted it.

Does the Guggenheim do its job?

Wright intended the visitor to take a lift to the top of the single spiralling ramp and begin a slow descent, admiring the paintings on the inner walls. These walls slope gently back, making the paintings seem still to be mounted on easels. A continuous band of skylights and artificial light sources illuminate the art treasures – works by modern masters such as Picasso, Klee, Kandinsky and Chagall.

Wright's Guggenheim Museum, New York, opened to the public in October 1959. The architect had been dead for six months.

To supervise the building, Wright took up residence in an apartment at the New York Plaza Hotel, redecorated it entirely and called it 'Taliesin East'. Before, during and after construction, a hot debate raged on the building's suitability for housing paintings. Some critics were awestruck by the Guggenheim while others believed Wright's design would always detract attention from the paintings themselves. This debate has never really stopped.

Two final resting places

In 1956, Wright visited the land of his forefathers for the only time, to collect an **honorary degree** from the University of Wales. Wright valued his **Celtic** ancestry highly and dwelt on it increasingly in his later years. In his *Autobiography* he wrote a kind of fantasy about walking through his family graveyard where ghosts urged him to look at the symbol carved on the gate. 'There it was in stone… Truth Against the World, the revered symbol old Timothy had carved there on the gatepost for the Lloyd Joneses. Strange… a new meaning… Why had I not seen it before? The truth to set against the woes of this world is Joy!'

Wright and Olgivanna (left) at a musical evening at home. Ten years after his death, Wright inspired songwriter Paul Simon to write, 'So Long, Frank Lloyd Wright':
Architects may come and
Architects may go and
Never change your point of view.
When I run dry
I stop awhile and think of you.

Wright died peacefully in 1959 after an operation on his intestines. He was buried at Taliesin, but 26 years later, after the death of Olgivanna, his remains were **exhumed**, cremated and then transported west to Arizona to be with those of his third wife. 'Daddy gets cold up there in Wisconsin,' his daughter Iovanna had remarked. Some members of his Wisconsin family were not so sure, and strongly disapproved of disturbing him. Even in death, Wright could cause controversy.

FRANK LLOYD WRIGHT: THE MAN AND HIS WORK

In the late 1920s, Isabelle Doyle worked at the State Bank of Spring Green. She also worked as a secretary at Taliesin in the evenings. One day, Frank Lloyd Wright swept into the bank in his smartest outfit, wearing a Stetson hat and swinging a cane. Ms Doyle remembered the bank manager looking Wright up and down and saying, 'You certainly look comfortable.' Wright replied, 'You could do this if you weren't so strait-laced.' And, looking down, only then did she realize that he was not wearing any shoes! That was Wright at his most typical: the self-conscious eccentric.

An ultimate nonconformist

'Whoso would be a man,' wrote the American author Ralph Waldo Emerson, 'must be a **nonconformist**.' Wright lived this idea to the full. Born into a family of religious nonconformists, he seldom agreed with the majority view in any other area of life. He had his own vision of how life should be lived – and of how buildings should be designed and built. It wasn't always a vision that other people shared or that he cared to explain. In her 1992 biography of Wright, Meryle Secrest wrote of his work: 'Nothing about

Wright (seated) at the hub of his home and business – the study at Taliesin – where he designed so many of his masterpieces.

> *'A great architect is not made by way of a brain nearly so much as he is made by way of a cultivated, enriched heart. It is the love of the thing he does that really qualifies him in the end. And I believe the quality of love is the quality of great intelligence, great perception, deep feeling.'*
> Wright, at the end of his life, addressing the Fellowship at Taliesin.

Wright's buildings is conceivable at first glance, as if he felt that the hidden treasure at their core was a prize that must be won.'

Wright's vision required a huge amount of self-belief, especially when the chips were down. In fact, the stiffer the challenge, the more inspired he became to succeed. Then he could draw not only on his great talent, but also on his great energy – his relish for what he called 'the old gospel of hard work: adding tired to tired'. As he grew older, none of this changed. 'A creative life is a young one,' he said on his eightieth birthday, adding, with his usual sense of mischief: 'What makes you think that 80 is old?'

Ignoring 'the next thing'

The philosopher Bertrand Russell once wrote, 'As men grow more industrialized and regimented, the kind of delight that is common in children becomes impossible to adults, because they are always thinking of the next thing, and cannot let themselves be absorbed in the moment. This habit of thinking of the 'next thing' is more fatal to any kind of **aesthetic** excellence than any other habit of mind.'

Wright refused ever to look too far ahead. This got him into some financial and personal troubles. But he never lost his capacity to be 'absorbed in the moment', to express himself joyfully through his marvellous gift of creativity. 'The purpose of the universe is to play,' he said. 'The artists know that, and they know that play and art creation are different names for the same thing.'

FRANK LLOYD WRIGHT'S INFLUENCE

Frank Lloyd Wright worked tirelessly to create an architecture that was truly American, born of the culture and landscape of the country. He helped to give other architects the confidence to design in an **indigenous** American style. But through his designs, his writings, his talks, and the hundreds of apprentices who passed through the Fellowship, his ideas became influential all over the world. Throughout his career he had critics as well as fans. Some believed that after World War I his '**organic**' concepts had no further place in modern architecture, others felt his work was too 'personal'. Lewis Mumford thought Wright's passion for unity could be overwhelming; when he took a **motif** like a triangle and applied it to every aspect of his design: 'One's eye vainly seeks relief from this almost obsessive repetition.'

Some even poured scorn on Wright's apprenticeship system at Taliesin: 'Never,' went a joke, 'have so many people spent so

Wright's Marin County Civic Center of 1957 (right) was an attempt to blend government buildings with Californian hills, making full use of 20th-century technology and materials. To him, '**classic**' structures like the Lincoln Memorial (left) had no place in the USA, because it 'is related to the toga and the civilization that wore it'.

Wright's influence on the Europeans

Wright could not be ignored by European architects of the International Style (see page 32), even though their ideas could seem very different from his. The Swiss architect Le Corbusier wrote in 1925: 'the sight of several [of his] houses in 1914 strongly impressed me. I was totally unaware that there could be in America an architectural manifestation so purified and so innovative... Wright introduced order, and he imposed himself as an architect.' In Vienna, Richard Neutra claimed that, 'Whoever he was, Frank Lloyd Wright, the man far away, had done something momentous and rich in meaning.' Some critics also believed Wright's work helped pave the way for the 'Art Deco' style launched in Paris in 1925, which featured geometrical and angular designs and decorative motifs.

much time making a very few people comfortable.' But despite his unconventional methods, Wright took his teaching seriously. Olgivanna, with an eye to the future, made sure of that. 'It is not enough to build monuments, Frank,' she once told him, 'now you must build the builders of monuments.'

Passing on the principles

Few critics can deny that Wright's theories had a major effect on modern architecture and the way it is seen. His principles, rather than any particular style, have had an enormous impact. In 1940 the *New York Times* remarked that his main ideas, first expressed in the late 1800s, were both ahead of their time and timeless: 'Simplicity, **repose**, individuality; adaptation of the building to its owner, its purposes and its environment; bringing out "the nature of the materials"; use of the machine to do the work it can do well; sincerity, integrity – these are virtues of architecture now as they were, or should have been, then.'

As for Wright himself, he rarely doubted his own significance. Once, in a court of law, he referred to himself as the world's greatest architect. When someone pointed out that this was not very modest, he replied, 'Well, I was under oath, wasn't I?'

TIMELINE

1867   Wright born in Richland Center, Wisconsin, on 8 June.

1869–77   Wright family constantly on the move as father seeks work.

1878   Family moves to Madison, Wisconsin. Wright starts to spend summers at James Lloyd Jones' farm near Spring Green.

1885   Wright's parents divorce and father leaves Madison. Wright takes part-time **draftsman**'s job with engineer Allan D. Conover.

1886   Attends University of Wisconsin as a special student.

1887–89   Leaves Madison for Chicago, becoming a designer for J.L. Silsbee, then goes to work for firm of Adler and Sullivan.

1889   Marries Catherine 'Kitty' Lee Tobin. Designs their own home in Oak Park outside Chicago.

1890   First son Lloyd born.

1892   Son John born.

1893   Wright leaves Adler and Sullivan to open his own **practice**. Designs house and stables for William H. Winslow, River Forest, Illinois.

1894   First exhibition of Wright's work held at Chicago Architectural Club. Daughter Catherine born.

1895   Son David born.

1896   Wright writes the lecture 'Architecture, Architect and Client'. Designs 'Romeo and Juliet' Windmill Tower, Spring Green, Wisconsin.

1897   Moves offices to Steinway Hall, Chicago.

1898   Daughter Frances born.

1901   Wright delivers his lecture 'The Art and Craft of the Machine' in Chicago. Designs house for Ward W. Willits at Highland Park, Illinois.

1902   Meets future clients and patrons, William E. and Darwin D. Martin; designs house for Susan Lawrence Dana at Springfield, Illinois.

1903   Son Llewellyn born.

1904   Wright's father dies. Wright does not attend the funeral. Designs Unity Temple at Oak Park, Illinois. Also designs the Larkin Building (Buffalo, New York), considered by many to be the first modern office building in the USA.

1905	Wright and Kitty make first trip to Japan, and Wright begins collecting Japanese prints.
1906	Designs house for Frederick C. Robie in Chicago.
1908	Designs Avery Coonley House, Riverside, Illinois.
1909	Abruptly leaves practice and family to travel in Europe with Mamah Borthwick Cheney; works on Wasmuth **Portfolio** of his work, published in Berlin to international acclaim. Inspired in Italy to build Taliesin when back in USA.
1911	Begins to build Taliesin, near Spring Green, Wisconsin.
1912	Publishes *The Japanese Print: An Interpretation*.
1913	Visits Japan to secure **commission** for Imperial Hotel, Tokyo. Designs Midway Gardens, Illinois.
1914	Mamah Cheney killed as servant destroys Taliesin in Wright's absence; rebuilding begins after a month. Wright meets Miriam Noel.
1916	Wright travels to Japan with Miriam and opens office in Tokyo to supervise construction of Imperial Hotel.
1917	Designs Hollyhock House for Aline Barnsdall, Los Angeles, and pursues further commissions in southern California.
1922	Returns from Japan and opens Los Angeles office. Wright and Kitty are divorced.
1923	Wright's mother dies; Imperial Hotel survives major Tokyo earthquake; Wright marries Miriam Noel. Designs house for John Storer in Los Angeles.
1924	Wright and Miriam separate. Wright meets Olgivanna Lazovich.
1925	Second fire at Taliesin, followed by rebuilding. Wright and Olgivanna have daughter Iovanna.
1926	Bank of Wisconsin takes ownership of Taliesin, to cover Wright's debts. Wright starts work on his *Autobiography*.
1927	Wright and Miriam divorce; Wright and Olgivanna spend winter in Arizona as he works on Arizona Biltmore Hotel.
1928	Marries Olgivanna.
1930	Delivers the Kahn lectures at Princeton University (published as *Modern Architecture* in 1931).

1931 Exhibition of Wright's life work travels to New York, Amsterdam, Berlin, Frankfurt, Brussels, Milwaukee, Eugene and Chicago.

1932 Founds the Taliesin Fellowship and begins work on building Fellowship Complex at Taliesin; *An Autobiography* and *The Disappearing City* are published; Wright's work is included in the 'International Style Exhibition' at the New York Museum of Modern Art.

1933 Designs house for Malcolm Willey, Minneapolis, Minnesota.

1934 Wright and apprentices begin Broadacre City project model. Founding of *Taliesin* magazine to be published by Taliesin Press.

1935 Designs Fallingwater house for Edgar J. Kaufmann at Bear Run, Pennsylvania.

1937 Begins design and construction of Taliesin West, near Phoenix, Arizona; designs Wingspread House for Herbert F. Johnson in Racine, Wisconsin.

1938 Produces Master Plan for Florida Southern College, Lakeland.

1939 Completes Johnson Wax Administration Building in Racine, Wisconsin.
Outbreak of World War II.

1940 'The Work of Frank Lloyd Wright', a major retrospective exhibition, is held at the New York Museum of Modern Art. Wright founds the **Frank Lloyd Wright Foundation**.

1941 Made honorary member of the Royal Institute of British Architects, and receives Royal Gold Medal for Architecture from King George VI.

1942 Made honorary member of National Academy of Architects, Uruguay; Wright designs Industrial Arts Building, Florida and Southern College in Lakeland, Florida.

1943 Makes original design for Solomon R. Guggenheim Museum, New York.

1945 Designs Administration Building at Florida Southern College in Lakeland, Florida.

1946 Wright's stepdaughter Svetlana dies in car accident. Wright designs Unitarian Meeting House in Shorewood Hills, Wisconsin, and Johnson Wax Research Tower, Racine, Wisconsin.

1947 Receives **honorary doctorate** of fine arts from Princeton University.

1948 January issue of *Architectural Forum* is dedicated to Wright's work.

1949 Wright publishes *Genius and the Mobocracy* about his **mentor** Louis Sullivan; Wright made honorary member of American National Institute of Arts and Letters and awarded the Gold Medal of the American Institute of Architects.

1950 Awarded honorary doctorate of law by Florida Southern College, Lakeland.

1951 Wright and his apprentices design and construct exhibition called 'Sixty Years of Living Architecture', which opens in Florence, Italy.

1953 Wright publishes *The Future of Architecture*.
Made honorary member of the National Academy of Finland.

1954 Designs Beth Sholom Synagogue, Elkins Park, Pennsylvania. Hotel Plaza Apartment in New York is remodelled for Wright to live in.

1955 Opens office and residence in New York City: 'Taliesin East' at the Plaza Hotel; Wright designs Dallas Theatre Center in Texas.

1956 Publishes *The Story of the Tower*; October 17 is declared Frank Lloyd Wright Day in Chicago; Wright presents 'Mile High Illinois' at Chicago exhibition; visits Wales to collect an honorary degree; final revised scheme for Guggenheim Museum is approved and construction work begins.

1957 Travels to Baghdad, Iraq to discuss new cultural centre project; Wright designs Marin County Civic Center and Post Office at San Rafael in California.

1958 Publishes *The Living City*; he is awarded the Gold Medal by the National Concrete Masonry Association.

1959 Starts work on a history of architecture for teenagers, *The Wonderful World of Architecture*.
He dies on 9 April before finishing it.
The Guggenheim Museum opens in October.

GLOSSARY

abstraction an artistic representation of a thing which does not try to show it realistically

aesthetic to do with the appreciation of beauty

Balkans south-eastern part of Europe including Greece, Bosnia, Croatia, Bulgaria and Albania

cantilever long bracket or projecting beam fixed at one end, for example in a wall, to support a structure, such as a balcony

Celtic name for the original people who inhabited Scotland, Ireland, Wales, Cornwall and Brittany, and their culture

citation an official recognition of achievement, such as a descriptive note accompanying the announcement of an award

civil engineer someone who plans and builds railways, docks and many other public buildings and structures

classical characteristic of the art of Ancient Greece or Rome

commission agreement by a person to pay for a job to be done

coping top course of stone in a wall

countenance appearance, or expression of the face

curvilinear consisting of curved lines

decentralized to move things away from the centre, for example, moving shops out of a city centre

democracy/democratic type of society where everyone has a say in the running of the country by electing the government

Depression economic slump that began in 1929 when money dropped in value leading to mass unemployment

draftsman someone who makes drawings or sketches, in this case of buildings

entablature part of a building running along the top of a series of columns

evolutionary developing smoothly from earlier forms

exhume to dig up from a place of burial

filament thread, fibre

form shape and structure

Frank Lloyd Wright Foundation established by Wright in 1940 following the formation of the Taliesin Fellowship in 1932. The Foundation preserves Wright's works and continues to provide opportunities to study organic architecture.

honorary degree/doctorate educational qualifications offered out of respect, without the receiver having to take examinations

indigenous belonging to or originally inhabiting a region or locality

indiscernible invisible, impossible to make out

Industrial Revolution name given to the period between about 1750 and 1850 in which machinery came to replace human labour

maxim short saying expressing a general truth or rule of conduct

mentor experienced and trusted adviser

metropolis chief city of a region

motif repeated theme, subject or figure

mythologize make into something larger than life

nonconformist not believing or behaving like most others, often in religious matters

open-plan building with few interior walls

organic in architecture, a building that fits in naturally with its natural surroundings, yet forms a complete whole within itself

pilasters rectangular columns engaged with a wall surface

plasticity/plastic (in architectural sense) fluidity, lack of straight lines and right angles

portfolio published edition of an architect's plans, drawings and so on

post-and-beam traditional, non-plastic, form of building, with vertical elements supporting horizontal parts

practice professional business or firm

prairie treeless stretch of grassland

quintessential purest or most typical form of something

radical extreme, wanting big, complete changes

repose rest, relaxation

resuscitation revival

settlement in a divorce, an agreed financial arrangement

shingle rectangular slip of wood like a tile, used on roofs and sides of buildings

solvent having enough money

stock company business company for a particular purpose contributed to by people who then have a share in its profits

storey floor or level of a building

stucco plaster or cement used for coating wall surfaces

terracotta brownish-red fine clay used to make building materials among other things

truss support for roof, bridge and so on

untrammelled unconfined, unhampered

Victorian term describing the period that covers the reign of Queen Victoria in Britain, which lasted from 1837 until her death in 1901

vista view, prospect

working drawings detailed drawings showing how builders are to construct a building

PLACES OF INTEREST AND FURTHER READING

Places to visit

Illinois Bureau of Tourism – Illinois boasts the largest collection of surviving buildings by Wright. Visiting details can be obtained from the Bureau of Tourism at www.enjoyillinois.com

Richland Center, Wisconsin – Wright's birthplace, a town which annually hosts a celebration of the architect's birthday (8 June). Debate continues over the exact site of his birth, but since the hills and prairies here inspired some of Wright's greatest work, the entire landscape could be regarded as a monument.

Solomon R. Guggenheim Museum, New York – Wright's final building and one of his most eye-catching. Check out what can be seen inside at www.guggenheim.org

Unity Temple, Oak Park, Chicago – Wright's most famous church, built in the area where he first found fame. You can take an online tour at

www.oprf.com/unity/tour

Websites

www.franklloydwright.org – a good place to start finding out more about Wright, this is the site of the Foundation formed by Wright himself; it includes a biographical sketch, chronology, photographs and information on all aspects of his work.

www.pbs.org/flw – a comprehensive overview of Wright's life and work, with excellent links to other related websites.

www.swcp.com/flw – the site of the Frank Lloyd Wright Building Conservancy, an organization devoted to preserving Wright's remaining buildings; it tells you where these buildings are located – and also which ones are for sale!

Further reading

Frank Lloyd Wright, Peter Blake (W. W. Norton, 1976)

Many Masks: A Life of Frank Lloyd Wright, Brendan Gill (G.P. Putnam's Sons 1987)

Frank Lloyd Wright's Robie House, Donald Hoffman (Dover, 1984)

Frank Lloyd Wright's Fallingwater, Donald Hoffman (Dover, 1978)

The Shock of the New, Robert Hughes (1981)

Pioneers of Modern Design, Nikolaus Pevsner (Penguin, 1986)

The Fountainhead (a novel based on Wright), Ayn Rand (New American Library, 1971 edition)

Frank Lloyd Wright: His Life and his Architecture, Robert C. Twombly (John Wiley, 1979)

My Father Who Is on Earth, John Lloyd Wright (Putnam's, 1946)

Our House, Olgivanna Lloyd Wright (Horizon Press, 1959)

Sources

Frank Lloyd Wright – A Biography, Finis Farr (Charles Scribner's & Sons, 1961)

Understanding Frank Lloyd Wright's Architecture, Donald Hoffman (Dover Publications, 1995)

Frank Lloyd Wright: Master Builder, B.B. Pfeiffer (Thames and Hudson 1997)

Frank Lloyd Wright – A Biography, Meryle Secrest (Chatto & Windus, 1992)

Frank Lloyd Wright, Daniel Treiber (Chapman & Hall, 1995)

An Autobiography, Frank Lloyd Wright (Longmans, Green, first published 1932)

INDEX

Titles in the *Creative Lives* series:

Hardback   0 431 13985 7

Hardback   0 431 13982 2

Hardback   0 431 13983 0

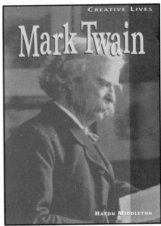

Hardback   0 431 13980 6

Hardback   0 431 13981 4

Find out about other Heinemann resources on our website www.heinemann.co.uk/library